W9-COM-775

71

J294.3 PEN

Discovering Religions

BUDDHISM

Sue Penney

RSVP

RAINTREE
STECK-VAUGHN
P U B L I S H E R S
The Steck-Vaughn Company

Austin, Texas

Published by Raintree Steck-Vaughn Publishers, an imprint of Steck-Vaughn Company.

Library of Congress Cataloging-in-Publication Data

Penney, Sue.
Buddhism / Sue Penney.
   p. cm. — (Discovering religions)
Includes index.
Summary: Explains the origins, evolution, teachings, and celebrations of the Buddhist religion.
   ISBN 0-8172-4395-X
   1. Buddhism—Juvenile literature.   [1. Buddism.]
I. Title.   II. Series.
BQ4032.P47   1997
294.3—dc20   96-3733
                                              CIP
                                              AC

Religious Studies consultants: W. Owen Cole, Steven L. Ware (Drew University)

Thanks are due to Anil Goonewardene for reading and advising on the manuscript.

Designed by Visual Image
Illustrated by Visual Image
Typeset by Tom Fenton Studio
Cover design by Amy Atkinson
Printed in Great Britain

1 2 3 4 5 6 7 8 9 WO 99 98 97 96

Acknowledgments

The publishers would like to thank the following for permission to use photographs:

Cover photograph by Graham Harrison.

Andes Press Agency p. 42; Aspect Picture Library p. 37; Christophe Bluntzer/Impact Photos p. 20; The Bridgeman Art Library pp. 28, 29; The J Allan Cash Photo Library pp. 13, 22, 25, 33; Circa Photo Library pp. 19, 43; Bruce Coleman Ltd p. 6; Douglas Dickins pp. 10, 30; C M Dixon p. 23; Anil Goonewardene p. 27; Sally and Richard Greenhill p. 47; Robert Harding Picture Libary pp. 31, 32, 35; Graham Harrison pp. 17, 18, 40; The Hutchison Library pp. 26, 46; Barry Lewis/Network p. 11; G Mermet/Impact Photos p. 44; Christine Osborne Pictures p. 45; Pana/Press Association p. 36; Ann and Bury Peerless pp. 8, 9, 38; Still Pictures p. 14; Topham Picturepoint p. 21; Zefa Pictures pp. 24, 34.

The author and publishers would like to thank the following for the use of copyright material: Columbia University Press for the extracts from Sources of Indian Tradition, Volume 1, general editor William Theodore de Bary, copyright © 1958, reprinted with the permission of the publishers, on pp. 19, 39, 41, 45, 47; Edward Arnold (Publishers) Ltd for the adapted extract, headed 'Buddhist thought', from Eight Major Religions in Britain, © Jane Bradshaw, 1979, on p. 43; Penguin Books Ltd for the extracts from the translation of The Dhammapada by Juan Mascaró, (Penguin Classics), © Juan Mascaró, 1973, on pp. 7, 11, 15, 17, 23, 25, 27, 31, 35, 37.

The publishers have made every effort to trace copyright holders. However, if any material has been incorrectly acknowledged, we would be pleased to correct this at the earliest opportunity.

CONTENTS

MAP: WHERE THE MAIN RELIGIONS BEGAN

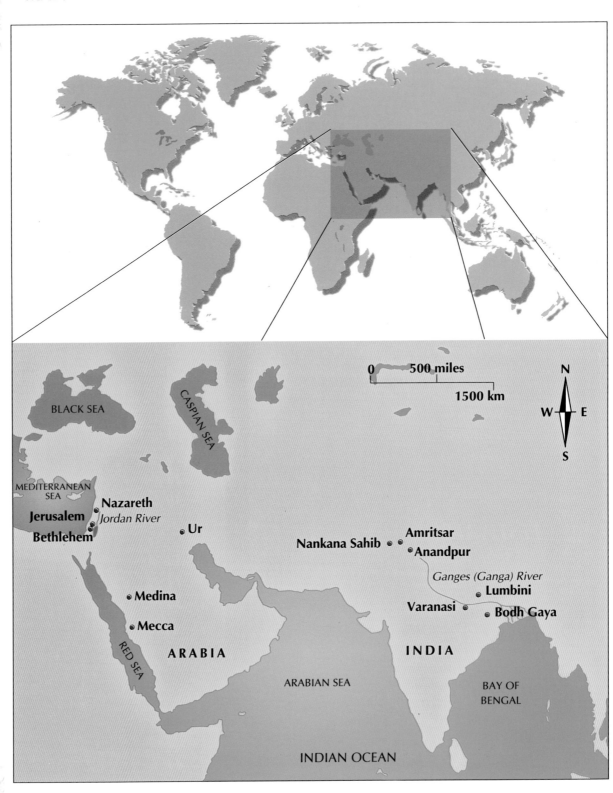

BLACK SEA

CASPIAN SEA

0   500 miles

1500 km

N
W   E
S

MEDITERRANEAN
SEA

Nazareth
Jerusalem
Jordan River
Bethlehem

Ur

Nankana Sahib

Amritsar
Anandpur

Ganges (Ganga) River

Medina

Lumbini
Varanasi
Bodh Gaya

Mecca

RED SEA

ARABIA

INDIA

ARABIAN SEA

BAY OF
BENGAL

INDIAN OCEAN

TIME CHART: WHEN THE MAIN RELIGIONS BEGAN

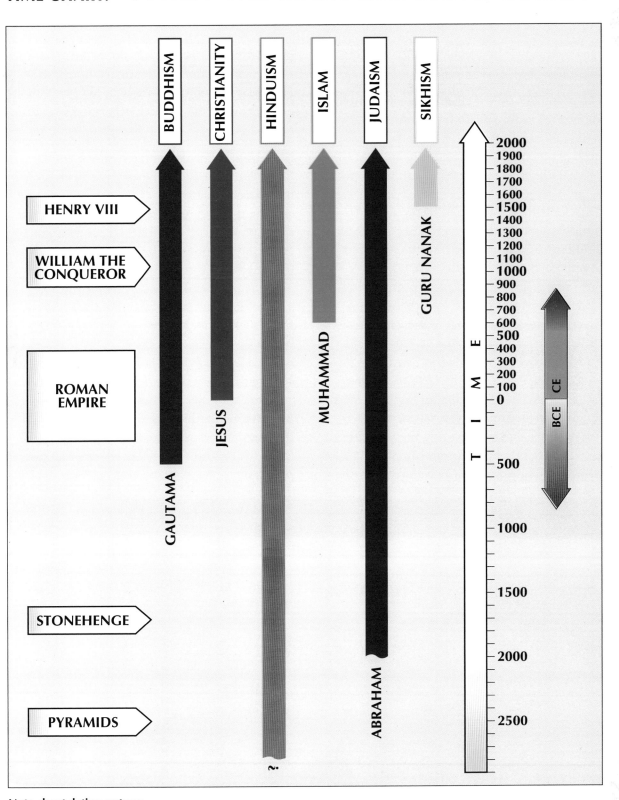

Note about dating systems

In this book dates are not called BC and AD which is the Christian dating system. The letters BCE and CE are used instead. BCE stands for Before the Common Era and CE stands for Common Era. BCE and CE can be used by people of all religions, Christians too. The year numbers are not changed.

INTRODUCING BUDDHISM

This section tells you something about who Buddhists are.

The present Buddhist teaching began in India about 2500 years ago. Today, there are estimated to be about 334 million Buddhists, most of whom live in Asia. There are about 590,000 Buddhists living in the United States.

What do Buddhists believe?

Buddhists follow the teachings of a man called Siddhartha Gautama, the **Buddha.** He lived in India in the sixth century BCE. Buddha is not a name, it is a special title. It means someone who has gained **Enlightenment.** Enlightenment is a special understanding— realizing the truth about the way things are. Buddhists believe that everything in the world is imperfect. They believe that in his Enlightenment the Buddha found the answer to why this is so and how it can be overcome. They believe that by following the teachings of the Buddha, other people can gain Enlighten-ment, too. Buddhists do not believe in an all-powerful God, and they do not believe that the Buddha himself was more than a human being. He was important because he achieved Enlight-enment and chose to teach others the way to achieve it, too.

Buddhists believe that unless they gain Enlightenment, when they die each person will be reborn. This belief is called **samsara**—a continual round of birth, old age, illness, death, and "rebecoming" or rebirth. Buddhists aim to break out of this continuous cycle and achieve **nirvana.** (This is sometimes spelled **Nibbana.**) Nirvana is the end of imperfection. Buddhists say that it is the "blowing out of the fires" of greed, hatred, and ignorance, which is followed by a state of perfect peace. They try to reach nirvana by following the Buddha's teachings and by **meditation.** Meditation means training your mind so that you can concentrate more fully. By meditating, Buddhists aim to control their mind so that they can go beyond thought. This is explained in more detail on page 22.

The lotus is a symbol of things that are pure and good.

Symbols of Buddhism

The **symbol** used for Buddhism is a wheel. This has eight spokes, which is a reminder that part of the Buddha's teaching was about eight ways of living. (This is explained in more detail on pages 16–17.) The wheel itself is a reminder of the continual cycle of birth, death and rebirth, which goes on and on like a wheel turning.

Another symbol that Buddhists often use is the **lotus** flower. It is a symbol of things that are pure and good. A lotus is a kind of water lily. It begins its life in the mud at the bottom of a pond and rises to the surface of the water to flower. The flower is not spoiled by the mud in which it grows. Buddhists say that in the same way, people can rise above the things which are not satisfactory in life and achieve Enlightenment.

The symbol of Buddhism.

NEW WORDS

Buddha "The Enlightened one."
Enlightenment Understanding the truth about the way things are.
Lotus A flower of the water lily family.
Meditation The mental control leading to concentration, calmness, and wisdom.
Nirvana (Nibbana) The stopping of greed, hatred, and ignorance.
Samsara The continual cycle of birth, illness, death and rebirth.
Symbol Something that stands for something else.

FOLLOWERS OF THE BUDDHA

The followers of Buddha Gautama are awake and forever watch; and ever by night and by day they remember Buddha their Master.

The followers of Buddha Gautama are awake and forever watch; and ever by night and by day they remember the Truth of the Law.

The followers of Buddha Gautama are awake and forever watch; and ever by night and by day they remember the holy brotherhood.

The followers of Buddha Gautama are awake and forever watch; and ever by night and by day they find joy in love for all beings.

The followers of Buddha Gautama are awake and forever watch; and ever by night and by day they find joy in supreme contemplation.

Dhammapada 21: 296–301

THE LIFE OF THE BUDDHA

This section tells you about the life of Siddhartha Gautama, the Buddha.

Siddhartha's early life

Siddhartha Gautama was an Indian prince. He was born at Lumbini, in what is now called Nepal, in the fifth century BCE. The stories say that when Siddhartha was born, his father asked eight wise men what he would become. All of them agreed that he would be a great man, but they said that if he ever saw suffering, he would become a great religious leader rather than a great ruler. Siddhartha's father ordered that no one who was sick or old should be allowed near the prince. Siddhartha grew up to be handsome and clever. When he was sixteen, he married a beautiful girl, and they had a son. Siddhartha was rich and powerful. It seemed that he had everything he could want.

However, Siddhartha became bored with his sheltered life in the palace, and one day he went riding outside the palace grounds. While he was out, four things disturbed him very much. He saw an old man—he had never seen old age before. He saw a sick man—he had never seen illness before. He saw a funeral, with the dead person's relatives weeping around the body. He had never seen sorrow or death before. As he was thinking about these things, he saw a holy man. The man was content and happy. He said that he had given up his home and his family to wander from place to place searching for the answers to the problem of suffering in the world.

Siddhartha was deeply disturbed by what he had seen, and decided that he, too, must try to find the answer to this problem. He left the palace that night, changed his royal robes for the simple clothes worn by holy men, and shaved his head.

Siddhartha's search for Enlightenment

For the next six years, Siddhartha traveled around India. He spent some time with two great teachers, then with a group of **monks.** He spent several years with five holy men who lived a very hard life, eating and drinking almost nothing. The idea was that if you force your body to suffer, it becomes less important to you. He found that starving himself did not help him to find any answers, so he began eating and drinking again. The holy men left

This old painting shows Siddhartha leaving his palace.

The Mahabodhi temple at Bodh Gaya.

him in disgust, because they thought he had given up. Siddhartha traveled on until at last he came to a great tree. Today this is called the **bodhi tree,** which means "tree of wisdom." He sat under the tree and meditated, and at last he gained Enlightenment. In other words, he achieved understanding of the meaning of life. Buddhists say that this is a feeling of total peace, when you can stop thinking about yourself and become totally free.

From this time on, Siddhartha Gautama was called "the Buddha." According to Buddhist teaching, having achieved Enlightenment, Siddhartha could have left Earth, but he chose not to do this. He believed that his knowledge should be passed on to others, so he spent the rest of his life teaching other people about the right ways to live. He passed away (Buddhists do not say that he died) at the age of 80. His body was **cremated,** and the ashes were placed in special burial mounds called **stupas.** Buddhists say that the Buddha's passing away was when he entered **Parinirvana.** This is the name given to the complete Nirvana at the end of a Buddha's life.

NEW WORDS

Bodhi tree The "tree of wisdom" under which the Buddha achieved Enlightenment.
Cremate To burn a body after death.
Monk A man who dedicates his life to his religion.
Parinirvana The complete nirvana.
Stupa The place where part of the Buddha's ashes were buried.

SIDDHARTHA AND THE SWAN

This story shows how the young prince cared for all living creatures.

One day, Siddhartha was walking in the palace woods with his cousin Devadatta, who had a bow and arrows. A swan flew overhead, and Devadatta shot it. Both boys ran to where it had fallen, and Siddhartha reached it first. He drew the arrow out of its wing, and squeezed juice from some leaves onto the wound to stop it from bleeding. Devadatta claimed that the bird should be his, but Siddhartha said that since he had saved its life, the swan was his. Unable to agree, they asked the wise men in the palace. The wise men said that if the swan had died it would have been Devadatta's, but since it was alive it was Siddhartha's— a life must belong to the one who tries to save it. Siddhartha cared for the swan until it was well enough to fly away.

BUDDHIST TEACHINGS

This section gives you an outline of Buddhist teachings.

The Three Jewels

Buddhist belief is summed up in the words that Buddhists repeat every day:

> *I take refuge in the Buddha*
>
> *I take refuge in the **Dharma** (teaching)*
>
> *I take refuge in the **Sangha** (Buddhist community)*

These are called the Three Jewels because they sum up the most precious part of Buddhist belief. The Buddha is respected because he

showed the way to Enlightenment. The Dharma is respected because Buddhists believe that the teaching needs to be realized in one's own life. Today, Sangha means the Buddhist monks and **nuns** who offer help and guidance in following Buddhism. A refuge is a safe place, so when Buddhists say that they take refuge in these three things, it is a way of showing how important they are.

Dharma

The Buddha's teachings are the most important part of Buddhism. Buddhists do not believe that the Buddha invented the teachings, because they believe that they are natural laws that have always existed. (The word dharma means "natural law.") They do believe that the Buddha was the person who put the teachings in a form that can be understood by people in this age of the world. Buddhists believe that by following the teachings and realizing that they are true for themselves, they can achieve Enlightenment.

Enlightenment

Enlightenment means "realizing the truth." It is not the same as knowing things because knowledge can be taught. Enlightenment is different because each person has to find the truth for himself or herself. (It may help you to understand this if you think of learning to swim or ride a bicycle. You can be told what to do, and understand what to do, but you have to discover the knack for yourself.) Buddhists believe that when they reach Enlightenment, they can break free of the endless cycle of birth, illness, death, and rebirth. They can enter nirvana.

Girls worshiping at a temple in Myanmar (formerly Burma).

Buddhists at a monastery in Europe.

Nirvana

Buddhists say that it is not possible to describe nirvana. There is a Buddhist story about a fish and a turtle who were friends. The fish asked the turtle to describe what life was like on land. The turtle tried, but the fish could not imagine air, or trees, or grass, or anything else that the turtle was talking about. Buddhists say that trying to describe nirvana is like this. The only way is to say what it is not like. Nirvana really means "going out"—like a fire goes out because it has no fuel. It is not life, it is not death. It means being free of greed and anger, and the end of everything that is imperfect. It is the state where "you" does not exist any longer. For a Buddhist it is the only way to be really free.

NEW WORDS

Dharma The "natural laws"—teachings of the Buddha.
Nun A woman who dedicates her life to her religion.
Sangha A community of Buddhist monks and nuns.

NIRVANA

Buddhists say that it is not really possible to say what nirvana is like. The only way is to say what it is not. This is a quotation from the Buddha's teaching in which he described nirvana.

> *A condition there is, brothers, where earth, water, fire and air are not; where there is neither consciousness nor space, nor a void. Neither this world nor a world beyond are there, neither are there the sun and the moon. It is not a coming, it is not a going, nor a standing still, nor a falling, nor a rising.*
>
> *That is the end of sorrow. That is nirvana.*

Udana 8

TEACHINGS OF THE BUDDHA I

This section tells you about part of the Buddha's teachings.

After the Buddha's Enlightenment, many people came to listen to him teaching and became his followers. He taught for nearly 50 years before he passed away, and his teaching was passed down by his followers who learned it by heart. People in those days were used to learning things by memorizing. Not many people could read or write, and this was the usual way to pass on important teachings. The Buddha's teaching was about all areas of life, but it is usually agreed that it is summed up in three parts. These are called the Three Signs of Being, the Four Noble Truths, and the Noble Eightfold Path. Buddhists believe that together these three show the way to live. They are not separate ways to choose—they all depend on each other, and need to be followed all together. This section looks at the Three Signs of Being.

The Three Signs of Being

The Three Signs of Being are **duhkha, anicca,** and **anatta.** They are three of the most important words in Buddhist belief.

Duhkha

Duhkha is often translated "suffering," but it means much more than pain. It means things like being uncomfortable or bored, too. Everything that is unsatisfactory is duhkha. Buddhists believe that this means life is duhkha because there is nothing in life that is totally perfect. The Buddha said that no one can escape duhkha. His teaching was a way of overcoming it.

Anicca

Anicca means "impermanence"—in other words, nothing lasts. People, plants, even solid things like mountains are changing all the time. The Buddha said that because nothing remains the same for long, there is no rest except Nirvana.

Anatta

Anatta means "no-soul." The Buddha taught that there is nothing that can be called a soul. Instead, he said that people are made up of five parts. They have a body, they can feel things, they have ideas, they can think, and they can be aware of things going on around them. These five things make up each person.

This teaching was particularly important because it is connected to another Buddhist belief—the teaching about rebirth. All Buddhists believe in rebirth—the continual cycle of birth, illness, death, and rebirth called samsara—but they do not believe that a soul or spirit continues from one body to another.

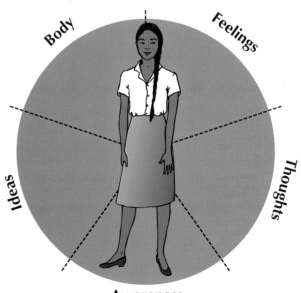

The Buddha taught that people are made up of five parts.

Instead, they say that what continues is the "life-force" which the person has made by the actions they have chosen in their life. Actions are called **karma,** and the Buddha taught that each person's karma affects their future lives. The force of a good life this time means they will be reborn into a higher life next time. A bad life means that they will be reborn into a lower life next time. All previous lives have an effect. Buddhists believe that the only way to break out of the force of karma is to follow the Buddha's teachings, and to meditate.

Worshipers at a temple in Thailand.

NEW WORDS

Anatta The belief that there is nothing that can be called a soul.
Anicca "Impermanence"—a belief that nothing lasts.
Duhkha Suffering, and everything that is unsatisfactory.
Karma Actions that affect future lives.

THE CHARIOT

This story is part of a much longer conversation between a king, Milinda, and a Buddhist monk called Nagasena. It is often used to explain the Buddhist teaching about "not-self."

Nagasena asked the king if he had walked to see him. The king said he had come in a chariot, so Nagasena asked what a chariot was. King Milinda was puzzled, and pointed to it. Nagasena asked again what it was—was it the wheels or the frame or the axle? The king said it was none of those things, but all of them, arranged in a certain way.

In the same way, say Buddhists, there is no "self" that makes a person. A human being is an arrangement of physical and mental parts that, when brought together in a particular pattern, make a person.

TEACHINGS OF THE BUDDHA II

This section tells you about the Four Noble Truths.

Most Buddhists would agree that the Four Noble Truths are the most important part of the Buddha's teaching. It was the main part of the first teaching he gave after his Enlightenment. He taught about the causes of duhkha, things being imperfect, and how it can be overcome. He said that when people realized the Four Noble Truths, they would be able to change their lives.

The First Noble Truth

Duhkha happens everywhere all the time.

The Buddha said that everything in the world is duhkha, because nothing is perfect. Every life has the karma, or force, from the person's previous lives. So being reborn means that everyone always suffers from the force of their previous lives. This means that every life has something wrong with it. Only when people have reached nirvana will they be able to overcome duhkha.

The Second Noble Truth

Duhkha is caused by greed and selfishness.

Everybody is basically selfish. We all tend to think about ourselves more than others, and we are always more concerned with what we want to do than with what other people want to do. This selfishness is a cause of the suffering in the world. The Buddha said that even being reborn is really selfish, and people should try to break out of the rebirth cycle.

The Third Noble Truth

Greed and selfishness can be stopped.

When you no longer want anything—when you can see beyond yourself, and what you are is no longer important—then you can leave suffering and imperfection behind. A Buddhist believes that you can only do this by breaking out of the rebirth cycle, which brings perfect freedom. This freedom is nirvana.

Buddhists say that all life is duhkha.

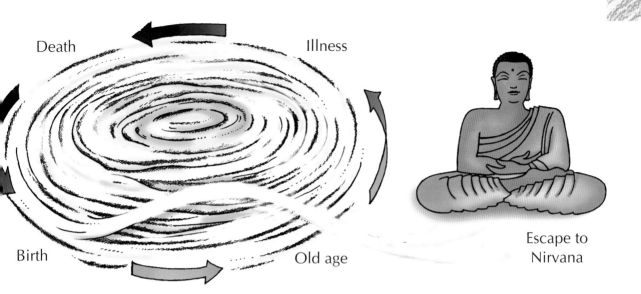

Death

Illness

Escape to
Nirvana

Birth

Old age

The cycle of life.

The Fourth Noble Truth

The way to stop selfishness is to follow the Noble Eightfold Path.

The Noble Eightfold Path is sometimes called the "Middle Way." It is the way of living that the Buddha said leads to nirvana. It is a way of helping people to realize nirvana by showing them how they should live. The Buddha said that it was as if people were trying to walk through very muddy ground. They can only be helped out of it by people who are standing on firm ground. The Noble Eightfold Path is the way to find this firm ground.

THE WAY TO LIVE

This teaching from the Dhammapada shows what the Buddha taught about the importance of following the right path.

Arise! Watch. Walk on the right path. He who follows the right path has joy in this world and in the world beyond.

Follow the right path: follow not the wrong path. He who follows the right path has joy in this world and in the world beyond.

He who in early days was unwise but later found wisdom, he sheds a light over the world like that of the moon when free from clouds.

The world is indeed in darkness, and how few can see the light! Just as a few birds can escape from a net, few souls can fly to the freedom of heaven.

Dhammapada 13: 168–9, 172,174

TEACHINGS OF THE BUDDHA III

This section tells you about the teachings called the Noble Eightfold Path.

The Buddha said that people should follow a "Middle Way" to nirvana. You should not live a life of luxury where you overeat and have too much of everything. But, just as important, you should not live a life where you starve yourself and punish your body. People who do these things will not find nirvana. The secret is to follow a middle path between extremes.

The Noble Eightfold Path

The path that the Buddha taught is called the Noble Eightfold Path. As its name suggests, it shows eight ways in which people should live. All of these things need to be acted on together. There is no point in following just one or two of the ways. All the parts of the path begin with the word "right." This does not only mean the correct way to do something. It also means the best possible way. The eight parts of the path are usually put into three groups. The first two parts go together.

Right viewpoint

A viewpoint is a way of looking at things. Unless you look at life in the right way, you will not be able to reach nirvana. This means following the basic teachings of Buddhism, for example, accepting that all of life is unsatisfactory, or duhkha.

Right thought

Your mind is very powerful, so it needs to be used in the right way. Thinking correctly about life leads to your being unselfish and caring about others rather than concentrating on yourself.

The next three ways show how Buddhists should behave when following the Path.

Right speech

Right speech does not cause harm to yourself or others. You should be kind and helpful when you talk to people, and not tell lies, swear, or gossip.

The Noble Eightfold Path.

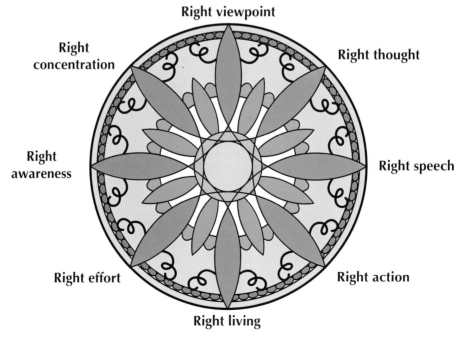

Right viewpoint

Right concentration

Right thought

Right awareness

Right speech

Right effort

Right action

Right living

Right living

If you want to follow the Buddha's teachings, you should work to the best of your ability. The job you do should be useful and not involve anything that harms others.

The next three ways are about training the mind.

Right effort

Training yourself to avoid bad things is part of right effort, but a Buddhist must also work hard to do good.

Right awareness

This means controlling your mind so that you can see things around you in the right way.

Right concentration

Training your mind to concentrate without wandering is achieved by meditation. When you can do this, you will become a very calm and peaceful person.

Lighting candles is part of Buddhist worship.

Right action

Right action includes avoiding killing anything and avoiding stealing or being dishonest. It also includes being faithful to your husband or wife and not drinking alcohol or taking drugs, because these things are harmful.

THE PATH

This teaching from the Dhammapada shows what the Buddha taught about the importance of the Noble Eightfold Path.

> *The best of paths is the path of eight. The best of truths, the four sayings. The best of states, freedom from passions. The best of men, the one who sees.*
>
> *This is the path. There is no other that leads to vision. Go on this path, and you will confuse Mara, the devil of confusion.*

> *Whoever goes on this path travels to the end of sorrow. I showed this path to the world when I found the roots of sorrow.*
>
> *It is you who must make the effort. The Great of the past only show the way.*
>
> *Dhammapada 20: 273–6*

THERAVADA AND MAHAYANA BUDDHISM

This teaching tells you about the two main groups of Buddhists.

All Buddhists follow the teachings of the Buddha, but like most religions, different groups do not agree exactly about their beliefs and the way in which things should be done. In Buddhism, groups are known as schools. There are two main schools. One is usually called **Theravada** Buddhism, the other is usually called **Mahayana** Buddhism. Both of these schools have within them smaller groups who emphasize particular ideas or beliefs.

Theravada Buddhists

Theravada means "teachings of the elders." Elders are respected leaders of a religion. Theravada Buddhism is based on Buddhist teachings which were written in the language called **Pali.** Theravada is sometimes called "southern" Buddhism because it is mainly found in countries like Sri Lanka, Myanmar (or Burma) Cambodia, Thailand, and Vietnam.

Theravada Buddhists emphasize the idea that each person must gain Enlightenment for themselves. No one else can do it for you. They believe that the Buddha taught people how they should live, but he was only a man. The only way he can help people to gain Enlightenment today is through his teachings, so Theravada Buddhists do not pray to the Buddha.

Theravada Buddhists think that the best way to live is as a monk or a nun. Monks and nuns can concentrate on their religion because they have no responsibilities, such as a family or possessions. Not everyone can leave their home and dedicate their life to religion, and Theravada Buddhists accept that this means monks and nuns may be closer to nirvana than other people.

Mahayana Buddhism

Mahayana Buddhism began in India in about 100 BCE. It is now more popular in the northern countries of China, Japan, Korea, and Tibet and includes many different schools of Buddhism. Mahayana Buddhism uses the same ideas as Theravada Buddhism, but in some cases it has changed the way the ideas are understood and explained. Mahayana means "great vehicle." This is a way of saying that there is room for different ways to nirvana. Mahayana Buddhists believe that anyone can reach nirvana if they follow the Buddha's teachings and ask him for help.

Theravada Buddhist monks in Myanmar (Burma).

One of the ways that Mahayana Buddhism is most different is the belief in **Bodhisattvas.** A Bodhisattva is someone who has reached Enlightenment, and so could enter nirvana. Instead, they have chosen to be reborn and stay in the world to help others to achieve Enlightenment, too. There are many thousands of Bodhisattvas. Mahayana Buddhists pray to them for help in achieving Enlightenment and for help with problems in everyday life.

An image of the Bodhisattva Kuan Yin.

BODHISATTVAS

This description of Bodhisattvas comes from Mahayana Buddhist teaching.

> A Bodhisattva will give up his body and his life, but he will not give up the Law of Righteousness.
>
> He bows humbly to all beings and does not increase in pride.
>
> He has compassion on the weak, and does not dislike them.
>
> He gives the best food to those who are hungry.
>
> He protects those who are afraid.
>
> He strives for the healing of those who are sick.
>
> He delights [gives joy to] the poor with his riches.
>
> He speaks to all beings pleasingly.
>
> He shares his riches with those afflicted by poverty.
>
> He bears the burdens of those who are tired and weary.

Tathagataguhya Sutra

NEW WORDS

Bodhisattva A person who has reached Enlightenment but has chosen to be reborn to help others.
Mahayana The "great vehicle" (school of Buddhism).
Pali An ancient language.
Theravada The "teachings of the elders" (school of Buddhism).

OTHER SCHOOLS OF BUDDHISM

This section tells you about three of the best-known smaller schools of Mahayana Buddhism.

Zen Buddhism

Zen is a Japanese word which means meditation. Zen Buddhism is most popular in Japan and Korea, and in China where it is called Cha'an.

Like all Buddhists, followers of Zen Buddhism aim to reach Enlightenment. Buddhists say that you cannot reach Enlightenment by thinking about it—you have to go beyond your mind to achieve it. Zen Buddhists have their own ways of trying to reach Enlightenment. They say that it comes as a flash of higher understanding.

Like other Buddhist monks, Zen monks live in **monasteries,** but their training is usually more strict than other monks' training. They meditate for several hours each day in a special room, using ways of meditating which are special to Zen. They meditate sitting in the lotus position, cross-legged with each foot resting, sole up, on the opposite thigh. One of the best-known parts of Zen meditation is the use of koans—meditating on statements that do not seem to make sense. One of the most famous koans is "Imagine the sound of one hand clapping." The idea is to make your mind stop its usual way of thinking, to shock it into understanding.

Pure Land Buddhism

Pure Land (Jodo Shu) Buddhism is a school of Mahayana Buddhism that is particularly popular in Japan. It says that the age of the world in which we live is so wicked that people cannot achieve nirvana on their own. The only hope is to pray to the Buddha Amida who is Lord of the Pure Land. This is a stage on the way to nirvana. A **mantra** used by followers of this school is "Nembutsu Amida" which means "I call on you, Amida." The ideas of the Pure Land school are not accepted by many other Buddhists, who feel that they do not follow the teachings of the Buddha Gautama.

The garden is an important part of a Zen monastery.

Tibetan Buddhism

The branch of Buddhism that developed in Tibet has many different parts. Tibetan Buddhists respect the Dalai Lama. They believe that he is an appearance of the Bodhisattva who is most important for Tibetans. There is a mantra that is like a prayer to this Bodhisattva. It is *Aum mane padme hum.* In English this is "Glory to the jewel in the lotus," but its true meaning cannot really be translated. This prayer and others are written on prayer wheels and prayer flags. A prayer wheel is a cylinder with prayers written on the outside or on paper rolled up inside it. The larger the wheel, the more powerful the prayer. Many temples have prayer wheels bigger than a person. As the wheels are turned and the flags blow in the wind, Tibetan Buddhists believe that the prayers are repeated over and over again. The prayers are a way of building up **merit,** which is the reward for doing good things. It helps you on your way to nirvana.

NEW WORDS

Mantra A sacred chant that Buddhists believe has special power.
Merit A reward for good actions.
Monastery The place where monks live.

WHAT IS AN ELEPHANT?

Buddhism includes many different schools of belief. This traditional Indian story helps to explain why.

> Once, in a village in India there lived five blind men. In the forest one day, they met an elephant. Each of them felt a part of it, and described what he felt to the others. The first said, "It's a rope"—he had felt the tail. The second said, "It's a tree"—he had felt the leg. The third said, "An elephant is a fan"—he had felt the ear. The next said, "It's a barrel"—he had felt the body. The last one said, "An elephant is a hose." All of them were right, because they had described what they felt—but they could not feel the whole elephant. Each of them knew only a part, because the whole elephant was more than they could understand. In the same way, the whole truth of "belief" is more than we can understand.

Prayer wheels and prayer flags at a temple in Nepal.

WORSHIP I

This section tells you about how Buddhists worship.

Worship often means praying to a God or gods, and for this reason many Buddhists do not like using the word. In this book, worship means Buddhists meditating and reading from the holy books.

Buddhists may worship on their own or in groups. There is no special day of the week when they meet for worship, but days before the moon is new, full, or at half-moon are important.

Meditation

For most Buddhists, meditation is the most important part of worship. They usually sit on the floor, often with crossed legs, and try to empty their mind of all thoughts. This means that they can begin to focus on things that are really important. The point of meditation is to rise above any worries you may have, and the world and its problems. It is intended to control and develop the mind. By meditating, Buddhists believe that they will become better people and will be able to achieve Enlightenment.

Group worship

When Buddhists meet for worship, it is usually in the **shrine**-room of a temple. The shrine is beautifully decorated and contains an **image** of the Buddha. An image of the Buddha is called a **Buddharupa.** Before they go into the shrine-room, worshipers will remove their shoes. Inside, there are no seats, so worshipers sit on the floor. Legs are kept crossed or pointing to one side, since it is thought to be disrespectful to point one's legs towards the image. Worshipers may greet the Buddharupa by putting their hands together in front of their chest or face, and bowing slightly. This is the

Meditation.

usual way of greeting anyone in many Eastern countries. Sometimes a Buddhist may touch the chest, lips, and forehead with the hands, to show that the body, the speech, and the mind are all joining in the greeting. They may bow or kneel, and sometimes lie flat on the floor. These are all ways of showing respect to the image.

The people offer gifts of flowers and light, by lighting candles or lamps. In a temple, monks usually carry out the formal parts of the ceremonies. The people watch and meditate, and repeat set words and chants after the monks. There are readings from the Buddhist holy books, and a senior monk often gives a talk. At the end of the ceremony, the people often stay and drink tea together. Tea-drinking ceremonies can be part of worship as well as a way of getting rid of thirst. People sit quietly, drinking specially prepared tea from beautiful ups. There are often flower arrangements. The idea is to be surrounded by peace and beauty.

Individual worship

When they worship on their own, Buddhists meditate and repeat important parts of the holy books. Usually these are chanted—a special sort of singing using only a few notes. They often burn **incense,** and offer flowers and sometimes food like grains of rice to the Buddharupa. They may light candles, which are a symbol to show the light of the Buddha's teaching. Theravada Buddhists do not pray as part of their worship, but part of Mahayana Buddhist worship is to pray to Bodhisattvas for help in their lives.

Gifts may be offered to the Buddharupa as part of worship.

NEW WORDS

Buddharupa An image of the Buddha.
Image A statue.
Incense A sweet-smelling perfume.
Shrine A holy place.

CONTROLLING THE MIND

Meditation helps the worshiper to control his or her mind.

> *The mind is wavering and restless, difficult to guard and restrain: let the wise man straighten his mind as a maker of arrows makes his arrows straight.*

> *The mind is fickle and flighty, it flies after fancies wherever it likes: it is difficult indeed to restrain. But it is a great good to control the mind; a mind self-controlled is a source of great joy.*

> *He whose mind is unsteady, who knows not the path of Truth, whose faith and peace are ever-wavering, he shall never reach fullness of wisdom.*

> *But he whose mind in calm self-control is free from the lust of desires, who has risen above good and evil, he is awake and has no fear.*

Dhammapada 3: 33,35,38–9

WORSHIP II

This section tells you about the places where Buddhists worship.

Shrines

A shrine is special to followers of the religion, and Buddhists usually worship in front of a shrine. Shrines are decorated and contain an image of the Buddha, a Buddharupa. They also contain holders for incense, and usually flowers and candles. There are also places where offerings can be left. Different Buddhist schools have different traditions about other things that may be found in shrines. For example, Zen Buddhist shrines may have offerings of tea. Tibetan Buddhist shrines have bowls of water in them.

Shrine-rooms may also be very different. In Zen Buddhism, rooms are usually very plain and simple. In some other traditions they may be quite highly decorated. A shrine may be in a monastery or temple, or it may be one room in an ordinary house. This is more likely in Western countries where there are not many Buddhist temples.

Monasteries

A monastery is a place where monks live. Buddhist monasteries are "open" because the monks do not live away from ordinary people. Many Buddhists who live near a monastery go there to worship and study. For many children the monastery is also their school, where they are taught to read and write by the monks. Some Buddhist monasteries are just one building, but most are like a small village. The most important room is the shrine-room, which is used not just for worship but for all important meetings of the monks. There are also huts where the monks live. This is explained in more detail on pages 40–41.

An important part of a Buddhist monastery is the garden. Many monasteries have a carefully planned garden with trees and shrubs. The trees give shade, which is important in hot countries, and the gardens help to make the monastery a place of peace and quiet. The plants are also symbols that nothing lasts, because they grow, die, and their seeds grow again. In countries where it is possible for them to grow, monastery gardens often include a bodhi tree. This is the tree under which the Buddha was sitting when he achieved Enlightenment, so Buddhists think bodhi trees are important.

A Japanese Buddhist woman worshiping at the shrine in her house.

The stupa at Bodnath, in Nepal. (The eyes are symbols of the all-seeing eyes of the Buddha.)

Stupas

Many Buddhists go to worship at important stupas. A stupa is a burial mound. Some are part of monasteries, but others are built at holy places. After the Buddha had passed away, his body was cremated, and the ashes were taken to eight different places. Stupas were built around them. Another two were built, one over the spot where the body had been cremated, and one where the container used to collect the ashes was buried. Ten stupas therefore contain remains of the Buddha. Later, many other stupas were built where people wished to honor special Buddhists.

HOLY MEN

This teaching is about holy men or monks.

The man who controls his senses, as a good driver controls his horses, is calm like the Earth that endures; he is steady like a column that is firm; he is pure like a lake that is clear; he is free from Samsara, the ever-returning life-in-death.

Wherever holy men dwell, that is indeed a place of joy—whether it is in the village, or in a forest, or in a valley or on the hills.

They make delightful the forests where other people could not dwell. Because they have not the burden of desires, they have that joy which others find not.

Dhammapada 7: 95, 98–9

25

HOLY BOOKS

This section tells you about the holy books of Buddhism.

At first, none of the Buddha's teachings were written down. People in those days memorized important teachings. However, soon after he had passed away, people began to think that it would be a good idea to make sure there was a clear record of what the Buddha had said. This was because his teachings were thought to be so important. A meeting of 500 Buddhist monks was arranged. All the Buddha's teaching was recited by the **Venerable** Ananda and the Venerable Upali, who were two of the Buddha's closest followers. All the monks repeated the teaching together. This way they were sure that everyone agreed.

This teaching was passed down by the monks. It was not written down for about 400 years, but in that time there were several meetings to check that it was still accurate and to organize it. The two most important collections of the

*Reading and learning the
holy books is important.*

Buddha's teaching are the Pali **Canon** and the **Sanskrit** Canon. They are called this because Pali and Sanskrit are the ancient languages in which they were first written, and canon means "collection of writings." The fact that Buddhist Scriptures are written in two languages is the reason why many important Buddhist words can be spelled two ways—for example, nirvana and Nibbana. Nirvana is the Sanskrit form, Nibbana is the Pali form. Neither form is better or more correct than the other. The Pali Canon was the first collection to be written down. It is also called the **Tipitaka,** which means "three baskets." It was probably given this name because the teachings were first written down on palm leaves, which were kept in baskets. The Tipitaka are the most important teachings for Theravada Buddhists.

The Tipitaka

The first "basket" of the Tipitaka is called the Vinaya Pitaka, which means "discipline." It contains the rules for monks to follow, with some stories and other teachings. The second basket is the **Sutta** Pitaka, which contains most of the dharma, the teachings of the Buddha. The most well-known part of this basket is called the Dharmapada. The third basket is the Abhidharma Pitaka, which means "higher teaching." It mainly contains writings which explain the Buddha's teaching.

The most important of these three is the Sutta Pitaka, because it contains the teachings of the Buddha. A sutta is a small piece of teaching. The Sutta Pitaka also contains stories about the Buddha, including stories about his previous lives before he was Gautama. The most important part is the section called the Path of Teaching, because this contains the Four Noble Truths and the Noble Eightfold Path.

Buddhist nuns in a Western country reading from the holy books.

Mahayana Buddhist books

Mahayana Buddhists also follow the teachings of the Tipitaka, but they do not agree with Theravada Buddhists about which teachings are the most important. Two of the most important teachings for Mahayana Buddhists are the Diamond Sutta and the Lotus Sutta. Mahayana Buddhists also have their own special texts.

NEW WORDS

Canon The collection of writings, the Buddha's teaching.
Sanskrit An ancient language.
Sutta A small part of teaching, usually the Buddha's.
Tipitaka "The baskets"—a collection of the Buddha's teaching.
Venerable Term of respect used for Buddhist monks.

THE DHAMMAPADA

The Dhammapada is one of the most well-known books of Buddhist teaching. This is how it begins.

> *What we are today comes from our thoughts of yesterday, and our present thoughts build our life of tomorrow: our life is the creation of our mind.*

> *If a man speaks or acts with an impure mind, suffering follows him as the wheel of the cart follows the beast that draws the cart.*

> *What we are today comes from our thoughts of yesterday, and our present thoughts build our life of tomorrow: our life is the creation of our mind.*

> *If a man speaks or acts with a pure mind, joy follows him as his own shadow.*

Dhammapada 1: 1–2

SYMBOLS IN BUDDHISM

This section tells you about some of the symbols that Buddhists use.

Like all religions, Buddhism includes many ideas that are difficult to explain. Using symbols helps to make things clear without having to use words. The lotus flower, for example, is often used as a symbol for Buddhism. (See page 7.) Flowers may be used as offerings at Buddhist shrines. They help to make the shrine attractive, and they smell pleasant. But they are also a symbol of the belief that everything is duhkha, because they die quickly.

The Buddha

Images and pictures of the Buddha often use symbols. There are thousands of images of the Buddha, and he is usually shown in one of three positions—standing, sitting, or lying down. If he is standing, he usually has one hand raised, as if he is blessing people. If he is sitting down, he is often shown meditating in the lotus position. If he is shown teaching, he is usually sitting with one hand raised. Sometimes the first finger of his left hand is pointing to his right hand, and the thumb and first finger of his right hand form a circle. This is called "Setting the Wheel of Law in motion." It is a reference to his first teaching, when he talked about the laws of life. When the right hand is shown touching the Earth, it is a symbol that he is calling on the Earth to take notice of his teachings. This refers to a story about his Enlightenment. Pictures and images of him lying down usually show him at the end of his life, just before he entered Parinirvana.

Whatever the position, pictures and images of the Buddha may show any or all of 32 special symbols that show that he was not an ordinary person. For example, there is usually a "bump" on the top of this head, which is a sign that he had special gifts. He is often shown with a round mark on his forehead, which is sometimes called a third eye. No one suggests that Gautama really had this, but it is a symbol that he could see things which ordinary people cannot see. He is usually shown with long ear lobes, which is a sign that he came from an important family. His hair is usually curled, a symbol that he was a very holy man.

This image of the Buddha shows several of the special features.

28

A mandala.

with eight spokes that shows the Noble Eightfold Path) is one of these mandalas.

Another important mandala comes from Tibetan Buddhism. It is the Wheel of Life. It is made up of several pictures in a circle. The monster that holds the circle is the Lord of Death. The outside ring shows the twelve stages that human beings go through from birth to death. Inside this is a series of pictures showing possible places of rebirth. In the center are three animals—a snake, a type of fowl, and a pig. These are symbols—the snake stands for hatred, the fowl for greed, and the pig for ignorance. Pictures like these show Buddhist teachings and are used to help Buddhists meditate.

Mandalas

A **mandala** is a specially designed pattern, made up of circles, squares, and triangles. Sometimes mandalas are just patterns, but others include pictures of the Buddha or of Bodhisattvas. The Wheel of the Law (the wheel

NEW WORD

Mandala A specially designed pattern.

THE BUDDHA'S FIRST TEACHING

This is the beginning of the first teaching that the Buddha gave after his Enlightenment.

Listen. It has become clear to me that the first law of life is: good must come from good and evil must come from evil. Everything in life is subject to this law. Water always flows downhill, ice is always cold, fire is always hot. Praying to all the gods in India will not make water flow uphill, ice become hot or fire

cold. This is because there are laws of life which make things as they are so that all that is done cannot be made to become undone. Prayers and sacrifices to the gods must therefore be useless. If all our idols have no power to change anything in the world, then they ought not to be adored. If a man does good, the result of his actions will be good, if he does evil then the result will be evil. The adoration of idols is wrong and foolish.

Samyutta Nikaya

PILGRIMAGE

This section tells you about important places that Buddhists visit.

Many Buddhists feel that it helps them to follow their religion if they visit places where the Buddha lived and taught. They may also visit places like the stupas where parts of the Buddha's ashes were buried. Journeys which are made for reasons like these are called **pilgrimages.** People have many different reasons for going on pilgrimages, but for Buddhists the main reason is that they believe going to holy places, especially places where the Buddha lived and worked, will help them in their own search for Enlightenment.

Places where the Buddha lived

The Buddha was born in a place called Lumbini, in what is now called Nepal. The site where he was born is marked by a simple stone pillar which says on it "Here the Buddha was born." This is now quite a difficult place to get to, but a small group of monks live there, and there are temples where people meditate.

Bodh Gaya is the place in India where the Buddha gained Enlightenment. Buddhists from all over the world visit it, and it is an important meeting place. A bodhi tree grows there that is said to be descended from the same tree under which the Buddha sat to meditate. Pilgrims walk around this tree, their heads and feet bare as a sign of respect. They often sit under the tree to meditate, and offer flowers and other gifts. There are many temples nearby, and places where pilgrims can stay.

Other places of pilgrimage

The Buddha passed away at Kusinagara in northern India, and many Buddhists visit the

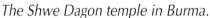
The Shwe Dagon temple in Burma.

Sunrise at Sri Pada.

stupa there. There are stupas in most Buddhist countries, but some of those in India, Nepal, and Sri Lanka are the most important. Many Buddhists make pilgrimages to them. When visiting a stupa, a Buddhist walks around it at least three times. This act recalls the Three Jewels (the Dharma, the Buddha, and the Sangha). Some temples are built where there are remains of the Buddha. The Shwe Dagon temple in Burma, for example, has eight of the Buddha's hairs. In Sri Lanka, there is a festival every year in the town of Kandy, where one of the Buddha's teeth is kept in the Temple of the Sacred Tooth. (See page 34.)

Some mountains are very important for Buddhists. One of the most important is Sri Pada, on the island of Sri Lanka. Buddhists believe that the Buddha visited Sri Lanka three times, and went once to Sri Pada. At the top of the mountain is a stone with what looks like footprints on it. Buddhists believe that these footprints were left by the Buddha.

NEW WORD

Pilgrimage A journey made for religious reasons.

THE IMPORTANCE OF BEING SINCERE

Buddhism teaches that it is important to be sincere—to live your life according to what you believe.

> *If a man speaks many holy words but he speaks and does not, this thoughtless man cannot enjoy the life of holiness: he is like a cowherd who counts the cows of his master.*

> *Whereas if a man speaks but a few holy words, and yet he lives the life of those words, free from passion and hate and illusion— with right vision and a mind free, craving for nothing both now and hereafter – the life of this man is a life of holiness.*

Dhammapada 1: 19–20

FESTIVALS I

This section tells you about festivals in Thailand, a Theravada Buddhist country.

Buddhists live in many countries. They follow the same religion, but of course groups of Buddhists also keep many of the customs of the country where they live. This means that the same festival can be celebrated in quite different ways in different countries.

Songkran

In Thailand, the festival of Songkran takes place in April and lasts for three days. It is the Thai New Year. Buddhists go to the local monastery to give presents to the monks. These are things like flowers, food, and candles. Everyone eats special foods and wears new clothes. This is a symbol that the new year is a chance to make a fresh start.

Water is important in the festival of Songkran. Boat races are held on rivers, and there are often water fights in the streets. During the dry season, fish are often trapped in ponds that form when the smaller rivers dry up. These fish are rescued by the people and kept until Songkran, when they are released into the deep river. Sometimes caged birds are set free instead. These customs are to follow the Buddha's teaching about being kind to all living things. Buddhists believe that by setting the creatures free, they will gain merit. (See page 21.)

Songkran ends at midnight on the third day. In temples and monasteries all over Thailand, a drum is beaten and a bell rung at the same time. This is repeated three times. When the sound has died away, the festival is over.

Wesak (called Vaisakha in some countries)

Wesak is celebrated by Buddhists all over the world. It is sometimes called Buddha Day. It celebrates the three most important events in the Buddha's life—his birth, his Enlightenment, and his passing away. Theravada

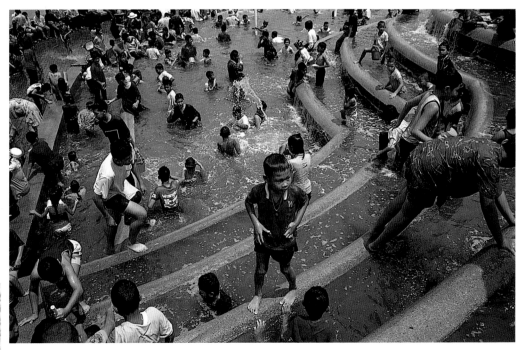

Celebrating Songkran.

Buddhists believe that these three events all happened on the day of the full moon in the month of Wesak (May or June in the Western calendar), so this is the date the festival is held. Many Buddhists give each other cards and presents to celebrate the festival.

In Thailand, people visit the temples and monasteries at Wesak. The monks give talks and preach to the people about the life of the Buddha. The shrines in the temples are beautifully decorated, and the people pour scented water over the image of the Buddha, the Buddharupa. At night, the image is taken out of the temple and put on a special platform. People walk around it carrying lamps, so that the Buddharupa is surrounded by light.

Pouring scented water over the Buddharupa.

Kathina

Kathina is a Thai festival which takes place at the end of the rainy season, during our November. It is a time when people can take gifts to the monastery, to thank the monks for the work they do during the year. It also shows that the people realize how important the monks are. The gifts are useful things like cloth for new robes. No monk is allowed to own things himself, so the gifts are given to the monastery. Giving at this time is thought to earn more merit for the giver.

WESAK

This account of a Wesak festival was written in the fifth century CE by a Chinese traveler called Fa Hsien.

Every year on the eighth day of the second month, they celebrate a procession of images. They make a four-wheeled car, and erect on it a structure of five stories made of bamboos tied together. On the four sides are niches with a Buddha seated in each and a Bodhisattva standing in attendance on him. There may be twenty cars, all grand and imposing, but each one different from the others. Then, on the great day, both monks and lay people come together with singers and musicians, making their devotions with flowers and incense. This goes on for two nights, with lamps burning and music playing all through the nights. Wealthy families dispense charity and give medicines to the poor and disabled.

FESTIVALS II

This section tells you about festivals in Sri Lanka.

Wesak

As in Thailand, the most important festival in Sri Lanka is Wesak, when Buddhists remember the three most important events in Buddha's life. In Sri Lanka, special ceremonies and worship take place in the temples. Streets and houses are lighted with lanterns. There are plays and dancing to celebrate the festival. Everyone makes a special effort to be kind to other people. Some people set up stands on the side of the road, offering free food and beverages to those who pass by. This is to remind everyone what the Buddha taught about being kind to others.

Poson

Poson is the month that falls in June—July in the Western calendar. The festival, also called Poson, is held on the day of the full moon. It celebrates the time when Buddhism was first brought to Sri Lanka in 250 BCE. Buddhists believe that the first Buddhist missionaries to go to Sri Lanka were a monk and a nun who were the son and daughter of the Emperor Asoka. (See page 38.) They were called the Venerable Mahinda and the Venerable Sanghamitta. A special play is performed in the town of Mihintale, where they arrived.

Esala Perahera

In the town of Kandy in Sri Lanka there is a Buddhist temple which was specially built to keep a **relic** of the Buddha, one of his teeth. This is kept locked away in a special **casket,** but for ten days every August the festival of Esala Perahera is held in its honor.

The most important part of the festival is a torchlight procession that takes place on the

Esala Perahera.

Dancing is an important part of many festivals.

night of the full moon. Over a hundred elephants take part in this procession. They are beautifully decorated and wear brightly colored cloths. The most important elephant, called Jayarajah, carries a special casket. This is an exact copy of the one which holds the Buddha's tooth. (The real one is far too important to be taken out of the temple.) Other elephants carry caskets with relics of other important Buddhists. The procession travels through the town, watched by huge crowds. This is a religious festival, but it is also a time for enjoyment. There are dancers, drummers, and fire-eaters. People light fireworks and burn incense and other sweet-smelling perfumes. Many people go to Kandy to watch the procession and to join in the festivities.

NEW WORDS

Casket A special container to store precious things.
Relic Old and treasured object, usually remains of a holy person.

THE IMPORTANCE OF LIVING IN THE RIGHT WAY

At Wesak, Sri Lankan Buddhists remember the Buddha's teaching about being kind to others.

> Hold not a sin of little worth, thinking "This is little to me." The falling of drops of water will in time fill a water jar. Even so the foolish man becomes full of evil, although he gathers it little by little.

> Hold not a deed of little worth, thinking "This is little to me." The falling of drops of water will in time fill a water jar. Even so the wise man becomes full of good, although he gathers it little by little.

Dhammapada 9: 121–2

FESTIVALS III

This section tells you about some of the most important festivals in Japan.

Japan is a Mahayana Buddhist country. This means that many of the festivals are different from those in Theravada Buddhist countries, although some still celebrate the same important events.

New Year

The Japanese use the same calendar as people in Western countries, so New Year falls on January 1. For Japanese Buddhists, the day before is more important. This is when the "Evening Bells" ceremony takes place. At midnight, the bells in every Buddhist temple are struck 108 times. This is a special number for Buddhists, because many Buddhists believe that it is the number of "mortal passions"—things like envy and jealousy. They believe that each ring of the bell drives out one of these faults. This is a time when Buddhists think about the things that have been wrong with their lives in the past year. They also think of what they can do to improve their lives in the new year.

Ringing the bell at a temple.

Obon

Obon takes place for four days in July. It is a family festival and, if possible, people go home to their parents to celebrate it. The festival reminds people one of the old stories about the Buddha. The story says that the mother of one of the Buddha's followers was rescued from hell by the Buddha. Some versions of the story say that the Buddha used a rope to pull her out, so in some places the festival is celebrated by tug-of-war competitions.

Mahayana Buddhists believe that the Buddha can help you in your life, and asking for his help is one of the purposes of this festival. They also believe that it is important to ask for his help for members of the family who have died. People visit the graves of relatives. In some areas, it is thought that the spirits of people who have died come back to the family home, so lamps are lighted to show them the way.

Obon is a serious festival, but it is also celebrated with fairs and dancing. One particular dance, where everyone joins hands and dances around in a circle, gives the festival its name.

Visiting the graves of relatives who have died is an important part of some festivals.

Higan

Higan takes place twice a year during the equinoxes. These are the two times a year when day and night are of equal length. It is also the time when the seasons begin to change. This is a kind of symbol because it reminds Buddhists that they need to change their lives, so they can reach Enlightenment. Higan is a time for remembering friends and relatives who have died. Buddhists go to the **cemeteries** to clean and look after the graves and decorate them with flowers. There are special ceremonies that Buddlists believe give merit to people who have died. This is important because they believe the extra merit can help them on their way to Nirvana.

NEW WORD

Cemetery A place where the dead are buried.

WAYS OF LIVING

New Year is a time for thinking about the way you live.

> *If by forsaking a small pleasure one finds a great joy, he who is wise will look to the greater and leave what is less.*
>
> *He who seeks happiness for himself by making others unhappy is bound in the chains of hate and from those he cannot be free.*

> *By not doing what should be done, and by doing what should not be done, the sinful desires of proud and thoughtful men increase.*
>
> *But those who are ever careful of their actions, who do not what should not be done, are those who are watchful and wise, and their sinful desires come to an end.*

Dhammapada 21: 290–3

THE HISTORY OF BUDDHISM

This section tells you something about the history of Buddhism.

The present Buddhist teaching began in India, when Siddhartha Gautama began teaching. He had reached Enlightenment but chose to stay in the world to show others the best way to live. His first followers were the five holy men who had spent years with him when he was still searching for Enlightenment. Before long, other people became interested in his teachings, too, and asked to join him. The group became known as the Sangha. This name is still used, but today it is used to refer to Buddhist monks and nuns. The Buddha's first followers included his own son, Rahula. At first, women were not allowed in this group. Only after he had been persuaded by his stepmother and his cousin, did the Buddha agree that women, too, could join. For the next 45 years, the Buddha spent his time traveling around India and neighboring countries, preaching and teaching.

Emperor Asoka

After the Buddha had passed away, his followers carried on his teaching, and Buddhism continued to grow. The teaching about respecting all life caught the attention of the Emperor Asoka. He had fought many successful wars and ruled almost the whole of India from 273 BCE to 232 BCE. He became unhappy at the suffering and death caused by the wars he had fought and **converted** to Buddhism. He tried to rule according to Buddhist teachings. He encouraged other people to become Buddhists and sent monks and nuns to travel from place to place teaching about Buddhism. Among these preachers were his own son and daughter, who took the teachings of Buddhism to Sri Lanka. Asoka ordered that stone pillars be put up where important things had happened to the Buddha. Writing on each pillar explained its importance. The emperor suggested that people should go on pilgrimages to these places. Asoka also had his policies for government written up in the same way. Many of these writings still survive today.

The spread of Buddhism

As Buddhism spread, different groups began to emphasize different teachings. This led to the development of the two main groups of Buddhists that still exist today, Mahayana and Theravada Buddhism. As Buddhism spread to

A stone pillar from the time of Asoka.

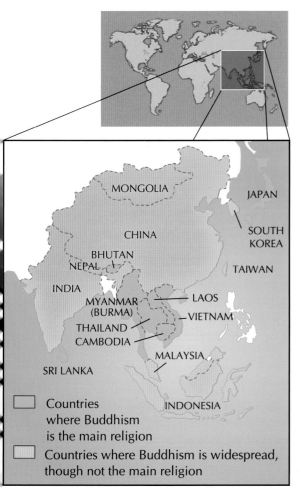

Buddhism in the world today.

different countries, people who became Buddhists did not leave behind everything they had known before. This means that Buddhist customs, particularly festivals, may be very different in different countries.

Numbers of Buddhists

Some "Buddhist countries" are ruled by governments that do not approve of the teachings of Buddhism, and this makes it difficult to know how many Buddhists there are in the world. It is also hard to estimate because many Buddhists do not attend temples, but have shrines in their homes. The official figure is estimated to be 339 million today, but other people suggest that the true figure may be closer to 600 million.

NEW WORD

Convert To become a member of a religion.

ASOKA'S WORDS

This is part of one of the rock edicts, or the policies for government that Asoka ordered to be written in stone and set up in many parts of India.

I am not satisfied simply with hard work or carrying out the affairs of state, for I consider my work to be the welfare of the whole world, of which hard work and the carrying out of affairs are merely the basis. There is no better deed than to work for the welfare of the whole world, and all my efforts are made that I may clear my debt to all beings. I make them happy here that they may attain heaven in the life to come.

Sixth Rock Edict

BUDDHIST MONKS AND NUNS

This section tells you something about Buddhist monks and nuns.

A Buddhist monk's work is his religion. Many Buddhist men become monks for a few months or years, so that they have time to study and learn about their religion. It is not expected that all monks will stay in the monastery all their lives. Especially in Theravada Buddhist countries, it is common for young boys to become monks so that they can be educated in the monastery. They may leave when they become adults. Women may become nuns, but this is not as common. Nuns and monks live in the same way, although the rules they follow are not always exactly the same. This section concentrates on monks because there are many more Buddhist monks than nuns.

A Buddhist monastery has small huts where monks live alone. The huts are furnished very simply, with a mat that is the monk's bed, and a small table or stool. He is expected to sit on the floor. There may also be a small shrine to help the monk meditate. Anything that is not essential, for example, pens and paper or books, are the property of the monastery, not his own. The only things that a monk owns are the robes he wears and a few necessary things. Most monks have two robes. The necessary things are a needle and thread to repair the robes, a razor, because most monks shave their heads, a bowl and cup for food and drink, and a special strainer. The strainer is to remove any insects from his drinking water. The Buddha taught his followers to be kind to all living things, and this means that Buddhists try hard not to kill anything, even by accident.

Buddhist monks spend most of the day alone, studying and meditating, but there is usually a time when they meet to study and meditate together. The Buddha taught that it is important to help others, and many monks spend part of their day working to help other people. This may be teaching, giving advice to people who need it, or some other form of service. As part of their simple life, their main meal is always eaten before midday, and after this time all monks **fast** until the following morning, although they may drink water, or tea without milk or sugar.

A Thai Buddhist monk studying outside his hut.

Alms

Monks are given their food and everything else they need by people living around the monastery. This is not begging because Buddhists are pleased to give to the monks. It is called giving **alms.** Buddhism teaches that giving to others is very important, and giving to monks is part of a Buddhist's religious duty. It also helps to earn merit. It used to be the custom for monks to go out on an alms round every morning, but today it is more common for people to bring their gifts to the monastery.

The five precepts

All Buddhists are expected to follow the five **precepts,** which are the guides for living as a Buddhist. A precept is a rule or guide to show you how to live. The five precepts are:

- not to harm living beings
- not to take what is not given
- to avoid improper sexual activity
- not to take part in improper speech
- to avoid alcohol and the misuse of drugs

When a Buddhist becomes a monk or nun, these rules are followed more strictly. For example, all sexual relationships are forbidden, and a Buddhist monk should not even be alone in the same room with a woman. There are also five extra precepts that all monks and nuns and some Buddhists who are not monks or nuns choose to follow. They agree not to:

- eat after midday
- attend music or dancing
- use perfume or jewelry
- sleep on a soft bed
- accept gifts of money

There are also rules of the monastery which monks and nuns must keep. The rules tend to be more strict in Theravada Buddhist countries.

NEW WORDS

Alms The necessities, including food, given to monks.
Fast To do without food and drink for religious reasons.
Precept A rule or guide for living.

BUDDHIST MONKS

This is part of a much longer passage describing what a Buddhist monk should try to be like.

> He takes only one meal a day, not eating at night or at the wrong time. He will not watch shows or attend fairs with song, dance and music. He will not wear ornaments or adorn himself with garlands, scents and cosmetics. He will not use a high or large bed. He will not accept gold or silver, raw grain or meat. He will not act as go-between or messenger. He will not buy or sell, or falsify with scales, weights or measures. He is never crooked, will never bribe or cheat or defraud. He will not injure, kill or put in bonds, or steal or do acts of violence.

Digha Nikaya 1: 4

BUDDHISM IN THE U.S.

This section tells you about Buddhism in the United States.

The first Buddhists to arrive in the U.S. came during the mid-nineteenth century from China and Japan. At that time economic and political conditions in these countries were not good. Many Buddhists settled around San Francisco or major ports along the West Coast. Some found employment in the construction of the first transcontinental railroad, the Union Pacific, which was completed in 1869. The first Buddhist temple in the United States was consecrated in San Francisco in 1898.

Some converts say that they like Buddhism because it does not ask them to believe anything they have not thought out for themselves. Others find that they agree with its teaching about the importance of taking care of everything in the world. Buddhism teaches about caring, not only for other people, but also for animals, insects, and the Earth itself.

Buddhist monks and nuns in the U.S.

Most Western Buddhists do not become monks and nuns, but there are a few places in the U.S. where Buddhist monks and nuns live. They live in much the same way as they would in Buddhist countries, spending their time meditating and teaching. They live very simply, and most do not have any belongings of their own. Some do not handle money. It is the custom for Buddhists to take food and other necessary things to the monastery. There are Buddhist priests who live a worldly life by being married and serving the people.

Retreats

Many Buddhists who are not monks or nuns go to the monasteries or **retreat** centers to meditate and study. A retreat is a special time when you leave your normal life behind for a few days or weeks. Buddhists at a retreat spend a lot of time meditating or studying. A retreat in a monastery gives people the chance

Inside a Buddhapadipa temple.

The Samye Ling Tibetan monastery in Scotland.

be with other Buddhists and live like a monk for a short time. They believe that this helps them become better Buddhists in their everyday lives.

In the U.S. there are several different groups of Buddhists, whose teachings are slightly different. Many Buddhists say that it is important to join a group whose teachings one agrees with. The first Buddhist group that established the temple system in the U.S. was the True Pure Land tradition (Jodo Shinshu). It is a tradition with priests that began in 1899 in San Francisco. The largest number of Buddhists follow Theravada teachings. The next most popular is the Tibetan and then the Zen tradition. There are also groups that aim to combine the most important teachings of Buddhism with Western ways of living. Most groups have temples, and worship is the same as it would be in a country where most people are Buddhist. People go there to meditate and listen to talks by the monks. In Buddhism there is no fixed day for worship in the temple, but people often worship on Sunday in the U.S.

NEW WORD

Retreat A special time of meditation away from normal life. Also the name of the place where this activity occurs.

BUDDHIST THOUGHT

This Buddhist question is one that is often used to illustrate the way in which Buddhist thought differs from Western thought.

> *There is a goose in a large glass bottle. The goose is growing larger, and must be released. How can it be freed without harming it or the bottle?*

In Western thought, this is likely to be seen as a problem, to be answered by ideas like making the goose smaller or the bottle larger.

The Buddhist answer is to ask how the goose came to be in the bottle. The answer is: "My thoughts put the goose in the bottle—therefore my thoughts can release it."

Special Occasions I

This section tells about some important ceremonies for young Buddhists.

Most religions have teachings about birth and death, but Buddhism teaches that the way a person lives is far more important. There are very few teachings in Buddhism about the beginning and ending of life because of the Buddhist belief that there is no soul. This means that—from the point of view of belief—birth and death are not very important. For most people, however, births and deaths are a very important part of life, and many Buddhists follow the customs of their country. This means that Buddhists in different countries may have quite different **rituals.** This section looks at the customs in Myanmar and Thailand, which are Theravada Buddhist countries.

Birth

The birth of a new baby is a time for happy celebrations. In countries like Myanmar (formerly Burma) and Thailand, it is the custom for the oldest members of the family to prepare gifts for the baby. A cradle is prepared, with clothes for the baby in it. When the baby is placed in the cradle for the first time, the gifts are placed around it. The gifts are usually "useful" things—if the baby is a boy, they may be tools and books. For a girl, they are more likely to be needles and thread.

The head shaving ceremony

The main ceremonies happen when the baby is a month old. The head is shaved because the hair is seen as a symbol of a bad karma in a previous life. Sacred threads are tied around the baby's wrists. Monks are often invited to this ceremony, and they may be asked to suggest a name for the baby. Food is always given to the monks when a baby is born.

Joining a monastery

Many Buddhist boys join a monastery at least for a few months. This often happens when they are in their teens or their early twenties, but in Burma and Thailand almost all boys join

A Buddhist monk school in Thailand.

Many Buddhist boys enter a monastery to be taught by the monks.

when they are ten or even younger. A boy who joins the monastery at this age is not expected to stay there all his life. Many boys stay for a short time, from a few weeks to a few years, so that they can be educated by the monks.

The **ordination** ceremony when a boy becomes a monk is one of the most important Buddhist ceremonies. In Myanmar, the boy acts out the story of how Siddhartha Gautama left his comfortable palace and became a wandering monk. There are special ceremonies. The boy's head is shaved (most monks have shaved heads), and older monks help him to dress in the monk's robes.

NEW WORDS

Ordination A ceremony in which a person becomes a monk.
Ritual The usual "pattern" for ceremonies.

DUTIES OF A CHILD TO PARENTS

This teaching is about how Buddhist sons should behave towards their parents.

A son should serve his mother and father in five ways; having been maintained by them in his childhood, he should maintain them in their old age; he should perform the duties which formerly devolved on them [were their responsibility]; he should maintain the honor and traditions of his family; he should make himself worthy of his heritage; and he should make offerings to the spirits of the departed.

Digha Nikaya 3

SPECIAL OCCASIONS II

This section tells about Buddhist ceremonies for marriage and death.

Marriage

In most Buddhist countries, marriages are arranged by the parents of the couple. This is because they have had more experience of life, so they are thought to know best. It is also because marriage joins two families, so it is thought that the families should be involved in the decision. The parents usually arrange for their son or daughter to meet a suitable person. The couple have the right to say "No," but, if they agree to the marriage, astrologers (people who tell the future from the stars) will usually be asked to suggest a good date for the wedding to take place.

In Buddhist countries, the wedding usually takes place in the bride's home. The ceremony is usually performed by a male relative of the bride, rather than a monk. The couple stand on a special platform called a **purowa,** which is decorated with white flowers. They usually exchange rings, and the thumbs of their right hands are tied together. Sometimes their right wrists are tied together with a silk scarf, instead. This is a symbol that they are being joined as husband and wife. Children recite particular parts of the Buddhist holy books. Then the couple repeat promises that they will respect and be faithful to each other.

A monk may give a talk about the Buddha's teaching on marriage as part of the wedding. If this does not happen, it is usual for the couple to go to the monastery together before or after the wedding, and listen to the Buddha's teaching there. At the end of the ceremony, everyone shares a meal. The celebrations after the wedding may go on for several days.

Death

Buddhist funerals are dignified, or somber. But they are not sad events, because of the idea that the person will be reborn or may have gained Enlightenment at the very end of their life. A monk may give a talk about the Buddha's teaching on what happens after death, and the Five Precepts and the Three Jewels are repeated. The body is usually cremated, and the ashes are scattered or buried.

When someone dies, their relatives often give gifts to the monks. They ask that the merit they gain from doing this should be shared with the person who has died. They believe that this may help the person. For the same reason, Buddhists always look after graves very

A Buddhist wedding in Malaysia.

46

Buddhist monks at a funeral ceremony in Singapore.

carefully. At festivals every year, there are ceremonies to pass on merit to the person who has died. Some Buddhists believe that there are places where a person can "rest" between lives, so passing on merit to them will help in their next life.

NEW WORD

Purowa A special platform for marriage.

DUTIES OF HUSBAND AND WIFE

This teaching is about how husbands and wives should care for each other.

> *A husband should serve his wife by honoring her; by respecting her; by remaining faithful to her; by giving her charge of the home; and by duly giving her adornments. A wife should care for him in five ways: she should be efficient in her household tasks; she should manage her servants well; she should be chaste; she should take care of the goods he brings home; and she should be skillful and untiring in all her duties.*

Digha Nikayu 3

INDEX

The numbers in **bold** tell
where the main definition
of the words are.

© 1995 Heinemann Educational
Publishers